P's & Cues for Travelers in Japan

Also, How to Get the Most Out of Your Yen

by Boye De Mente

SHUFUNOTOMO CO., LTD.
Tokyo, Japan

Copyright © in Japan 1974 by Boye De Mente
First printing, 1974

Published by Shufunotomo Co., Ltd.
1-chome, Surugadai, Kanda, Chiyoda-ku,
Tokyo, Japan

Exclusive Distributor in U.S.A. & Canada:
Japan Publications Trading Co. (U.S.A.), Inc.
1255 Howard St., San Francisco, Calif. 94103, U.S.A.
ISBN: 0-87040-289-7

Second printing, 1974

Printed in Japan

CONTENTS

FOREWORD

The old saying "It's the little things that count" is especially true in traveling—and particularly so for Westerners visiting Japan.

The traditional life-style and attitudes unique to Japan gave birth to many customs and manners that are also uniquely Japanese. Without some knowledge of these distinctive features, the traveler interested in understanding and enjoying Japan is seriously handicapped.

Part I of *P's & Cues for Travelers in Japan* successfully bridges this culture-gap. It is not only a practical guide to the little everyday situations the traveler is most likely to experience, it also provides useful insights into the "whys" of typical Japanese behavior.

In Part II of *P's & Cues for Travelers in Japan*, the author presents invaluable, detailed information on how both foreign visitors and foreign residents can take advantage of "non-tourist" facilities and services to substantially reduce the cost of living and traveling in Japan.

PART I

Crossing the Language Barrier

Difficulty in communicating is the main source of the more serious problems experienced by travelers in Japan. These problems most often arise when the rushed visitor speaks hurriedly—usually in English and frequently with a strong accent—and mistakenly assumes he has gotten his point across.

Japanese tend to be reluctant to admit it when they do not clearly understand what is said to them (whether the speaker is a foreigner or another Japanese) because this would "inconvenience" and possibly antagonize the speaker—not to mention the "face" they might lose.

When there is any doubt about whether or not you have been understood, you can often solve the problem by printing what you want to say, since most Japanese can read English with far more fluency than they can speak or understand it. Simply asking a person if he understands—when there is doubt—is usually not enough. The tendency, again is for him to say "yes" whether he does or not.

Few, if any, of the problems that arise from language differences are insurmountable handicaps, unless the visitor deliberately chooses to be unsympathetic and contrary. But the problems, particularly those pertaining to transportation arrangements, are time-consuming and can be frustrating if the traveler is not prepared for them—and costly if he ignores them.

Of course, the traveler who stays on the well-marked "tourist trail" is least apt to encounter serious communication problems, while those who like to pioneer their own paths would be wise to brush up on their patience and pantomime.

How to Greet People Properly

Westerners in Japan, whether residents or visitors, are continuously faced with an awkward and sometimes embarrassing problem of how to greet Japanese friends and how to respond to introductions.

The problem is caused by the fact that for most Japanese, shaking hands is still an unnatural means of greeting, while most Westerners feel just as self-conscious and awkward about bowing.

The problem is not terribly serious, but it does act as a barrier between Japanese and Westerners, emphasizing to both parties how different their traditional life-styles are, and making it more difficult for them to establish a fast and comfortable rapport with each other.

Of course, many Japanese who have worked or studied abroad or otherwise associated with Westerners for years have fully assimilated the handshake into their behavior, and many of the people the visitor meets will be in this growing group.

For various other occasions, however, a few pointers can add to the confidence and ease of the traveler. After years in Japan, it seems to me that the best approach is to use a combination of Western and Japanese manners, depending on the circumstances.

If you are introduced to someone whose hand you cannot easily reach, or to a group of people, I suggest that you bow slightly from the waist and at the same time duck your head a bit.

9

In this case, the bow is not only a lot more practical and simple, it is also the "right" thing to do.

Older women, particularly, can be expected to bow rather than shake hands, unless they are very Westernized, which will be almost immediately obvious from their manner.

Then there are many cosmopolitan Japanese and experienced foreigners who combine the handshake and the bow, a practice that I recommend highly because it allows both parties to retain the flavor and feel of their own etiquette while meeting the other person half way.

The important thing is to be alert and not force a handshake on anyone who does not respond naturally to it; and be ready to bow when the occasion calls for it. As most Westerners are only too aware, the physical problems involved in shaking hands, especially with several people, often result in embarrassing situations.

The Japanese bow has a special advantage as more often than not it allows you to maintain your dignity.

Calling People Names

Westerners, particularly Americans, are often on a first-name basis within minutes or even seconds after they meet for the first time. This is *not* the custom in Japan, and the visitor can avoid appearing insincere and superficial by knowing something about the traditional Japanese use of names, and following established custom.

The Japanese are considerably more formal in the use of names than their Western counterparts, and the division between first names and last names is distinct and tends to be rigid.

There are four main categories of name-calling, and one or two sub-categories. The only group of people that always uses first names (and without the popular *san* suffix) are parents referring to or addressing their own children. Older relatives, referring to or addressing nieces and nephews use first names but customarily add the suffix *san* (which means Mr., Mrs., or Miss).

The second group among which first names are commonly used are close school chums who are in the same grade and are approximately the same age.

Among adults, women generally call each other by their first names only if they grew up together and were close schoolmates or if they are still young (in their late teens or twenties), work together in an "informal" place such as a restaurant or club, and are good friends.

Women who have lived next door to each other for a lifetime, been good neighbors and shared many intimate experiences, still call each other by their last names, affixing the title of *san* (Honda-san, Sato-san, Suzuki-san, etc.)

Among men, only the closest of friends call each other by their first names, and only then in very informal situations. In a business office, it is customary for last names to be used, even among co-workers of the same age and rank who have been working together for years. There are occasional exceptions to this rule, such as when older managers address girls who have been working for them more or less as private secretaries for a long time.

The Japanese tend to be exceptionally tolerant of occidental residents and visitors, and do not expect them to confirm to all the meticulous rules of traditional Japanese behavior. But, this is another occasion where with just a little foreknowledge and effort the visitor can demonstrate that he has enough respect and goodwill for the Japanese to know as well as follow one of their more important customs.

All you have to do to be safe is call everyone by his or her last name, adding the *san*, on all occasions except when young children are involved, in personal or informal occasions with unmarried girls and young boys whom you have come to know well, and with English-speaking adults who have adopted Western first names.

Becoming Handy with *O'hashi*

One of the first things you will be expected to do upon arriving in Japan (if not while you are en route) is to eat with *O'hashi* (Oh-hah-she) or chopsticks.

O'hashi are the traditional eating implements of Japan, Korea, Taiwan, Hong Kong, and of course China, and mastering their use is one of the most interesting challenges that face most newcomers to Japan.

While all Western-style restaurants in Japan provide diners with knives, forks, and spoons, traditional Japanese foods and generally all meals served in traditional Japanese settings are eaten with *O'hashi*.

Whatever the situation, you can request Western-type cutlery if you don't feel inclined to tackle chopsticks, but if you do take the easy way out you will miss out on one of the tangible pleasures of experiencing a foreign culture. (Metal tableware has been shown to impart an unpleasant metalic taste to the food it touches and to the tongue—something that chosticks do not do.)

Visitors will usually be confronted by three types of chopsticks. One type is made of natural wood and is primarilly used in restaurants serving Japanese food. This type is called *waribashi* (wah-ree-bah-she), and is usually partly joined at one end as evidence that they have never been used. The diner pulls them apart, removing any splinters that might result by rubbing the two sticks together.

The second type of O'hashi that you will likely

meet are larger than the *waribashi* and are made of heavy ivory. These are preferred by Chinese restaurants. The third type is made of lacquered wood or plastic and is used in private homes. The *waribashi* are discarded after one use, whereas the lacquered, plastic and ivory chopsticks are, of course, reused.

The proper way to hold chopsticks is a bit tricky for the first-time user—see the following sketch. The lower stick remains mostly stationary.

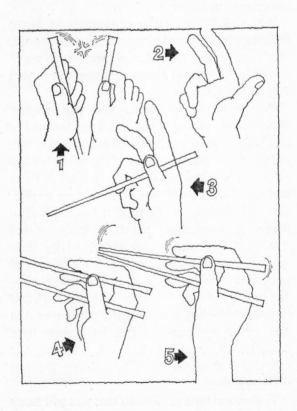

There are several DO'S and DON'TS in using chopsticks that are not essential but are good manners. Among the more important: do not stick the *O'hashi* into your food and leave them protruding, especially in rice, because this suggest death. Do not scrape off rice that adheres to the sticks.

When not in use, chopsticks should be laid parallel on an *O'hashi* rest provided for that purpose, or leaned against your plate or tray. When you are finished with the *O'hashi*, lay them across your plate or bowl. It is polite to rinse the sticks off in your tea cup before eating pickles, which are usually served at the end of the meal.

The Japanese develop considerable skill with chopsticks and become adept at using them to tear or render items of food that are larger than bite-size. In cases where this is difficult or impossible for you to do, it is acceptable for you to raise the piece to your mouth and bite off a chunk.

In this case, however, it is wise to hold your rice bowl under the piece while it is being raised to the mouth, as a kind of "back-up tray" in case it gets away from your chopsticks and falls. In some cases, the diner will rest the item on the rice while it is being conveyed to his mouth.

It is not considered the most genteel etiquette to bring the rice bowl close to the mouth when eating, but except on very formal occasion, most people do to varying degrees.

Most Japanese soups have various solid ingredients in them. To eat these ingredients without dripping soup on the table or yourself, it is necessary to raise the soup bowl up close to your mouth. Keep the business end of your chopsticks sticking into the bowl while you are conveying it to beneath your chin with both hands.

Of course, the *only* way you can drink soup is by raising the bowl to your mouth and sipping it. Again, it is customary to keep the business end of your chopsticks in the bowl while you are sipping.

Lacquered chopsticks are more difficult to use than the wooden ones because they are slicker. The most difficult of all to use are the heavy, sharply tapered ivory sticks favored by the Chinese. If you go to a Chinese restaurant and want the lightweight wooden ones, just ask for *wari-bashi*.

Remember, in informal situations it is alright to use your rice bowl as a "tray" to get food items close to your mouth. This can be invaluable when you first start using *O'hashi* because it not only helps you avoid accidents but also provides some insurance that you won't go hungry.

It is good manners to lay your chopsticks down and stop eating while you are being served. If you help yourself from a serving dish using your own chopsticks, strict etiquette calls for the sticks to be reversed and the opposite ends used.

Dining Japanese Style

Dining Japanese style, primarily means eating traditional Japanese foods in a traditional Japanese setting, but it can also mean eating anything, anywhere, in the manner that the Japanese do.

There are several things to keep in mind, depending on what, where, and with whom you eat. To bring up a number of points that are not so obvious, but come up frequently and are good to know:

It is not customary in many Japanese restaurants to automatically serve water to diners. If you want water you have to ask for it. Also, there is no tradition in Japan of making sure that *all* cooked foods are served piping hot, and many of the dishes that we serve hot may be served cold.

In resort inns, especially, about the only dish that you can reasonably expect to be served hot, if the food isn't cooked right on your table, is soup. Particularly when a large party is involved, such things as breakfast eggs and toast—all prepared for serving at the same time—frequently come in cold.

If you are going to a restaurant where all seating is on the floor, a tight dress can be a problem. If you have difficulty sitting for extended periods without being able to lean up against something, remember that many such restaurants have especially designed backrests for floor-sitting. These backrests are called *zaisu* (zi-sue) and can be asked for if one is not offered to you.

No kind of formal meal in Japan is complete without an alcoholic beverage, usually beer or

O'sake (oh-sah-kay), and it is customary to drink first and eat second. It is very common to see Japanese diners leave their food untouched for up to half an hour while they talk and drink. This can be disconcerting when you are out with Japanese friends for lunch and have a sharp appetite. It can be even more upsetting when you are invited to a typical Japanese banquet-dinner where the drinks flow freely before the meal is served and there are no hors d'oeuvres to help sustain you. On such occasions it is wise to fortify yourself with a small advance snack if at all possible.

The Japanese do mix eating and drinking, but not as freely as Americans. The one rule that used to be inviolate and is still pretty much observed is that drinking is permissible until you began eating rice. In the old days rice was often not served until you had finished the other main courses. Now it may be served sooner.

Another thing to keep in mind is when you are eating with Japanese friends, it is good manners to let the oldest person start first.

There is no scarcity of delicious food in Japan in almost any style you can imagine (in Tokyo alone there are over 30,000 restaurants and more than 50 different styles of cooking), but if you plan on getting off into remote areas, like climbing Mr. Fuji for instance, and are a finicky eater, it is wise to take along a couple of familiar snack items (fruit, cookies, sandwiches, etc.) which are readily available in the usual shops and markets.

Rice has traditionally been the main dish in all Japanese meals, and its preparation and consumption have become hedged in with many rules. One that you will encounter is that every grain of rice in your bowl is supposed to be eaten. If a Japanese sets his bowl down with some rice left in it, this is taken as a sign that he wants a refill.

There are several types of restaurants in Japan that it helps to be familiar with. These include the standard Western style *restoran* (res-toe-rahn); the ordinary Japanese style *ryori-ya* (rio-ree-yah); the *ryotei* (rio-tay) which is Japanese styled and features geisha entertainment; the *shokudo* (show-coo-doe) which is a short-order and cafe-type restaurant; the Chinese restaurant or *shina ryori-ya* (she-nah rio-ree-yah); and the *kissaten* (keys-sahh-tane), which features pastries, toast, light sandwiches, coffee, and soft drinks.

Minding Your Money Manners

Prior to 1868, the great mass of Japanese did not work for a money wage. Their needs were more or less taken care of by their employers, and the concept of putting a monetary value on their time and work, as is done now, was alien.

The privileged *Samurai* or elite warrior class, which made up a sizeable proportion of the population, felt strongly that talking about money or dealing in money matters was degrading.

This attitude toward money, which held sway in Japan for many generations, has not yet disappeared. It is still considered impolite to flaunt money openly or to hand anyone except a tradesman or clerk money that is not enclosed in an envelope or wrapped up in a piece of paper. Gifts of money are invariably presented in a special envelope made for that purpose.

Older Japanese especially are still inclined to feel that an ostentatious display of money is a mark of arrogance and contempt, and they may be insulted by such behavior. At the same time, they tend to look down on the type of person who will argue about the cost of an item—except in a recognized bargaining situation—or complain about a bill.

The Japanese who deal with Western residents and visitors daily, as well as the younger generation, have mostly discarded this traditional Japanese attitude toward money, but the visitor should keep the idea in mind and be safe rather than sorry by observing the old protocol.

The Tip Trap

The old Japanese attitude toward money is no doubt one of the reasons why they are sensitive about the practice of tipping. Tipping American style (directly to cab drivers, waiters, bellhops, etc.), is considered impolite as well as disruptive of both the ideal relationship between employees and guests, and interpersonal relations among employees.

The custom in Japan is for the management of hotels and certain first-class restaurants and clubs to add from 10 to 15 percent to the guest's bill as a "service charge." This is later shared among the employees in the form of general benefits, thereby "eliminating personal competition for tips and giving all employees the same incentive to do their best for guests."

About the only direct tipping that is done in Japan (the Government strongly discourages it on other occasions) is to the drivers of rented cars and to redcaps at train stations. Many restaurants, hotels, taxis, and the like have signs posted requesting that patrons refrain from tipping.

The personnel of the Japanese National Railways (JNR) are under orders to return any tip that is given to them.

If you get very special service from a room-boy or room-girl at your hotel or from maids at an inn, and want to show your appreciation despite the ban on tipping, you may have to resort to a gift of some kind rather than money.

There are a few exceptions to the above. When a Japanese throws a party for important guests at an inn or restaurant, he may have a cash tip delivered to the location *before the party* to ensure that he gets special service. Or the place will know from past experience that a generous "tip" can be added to the bill. Obviously this system is wiser than ours, especially if one is a generous tipper.

Surprising to some, perhaps, the no-direct-tipping practice in Japan does not result in any loss of service. In fact, the extraordinary service that one gets in Japan is a primary reason why the country is so popular as a travel area.

The Power of an Introduction

Interpersonal relations among the Japanese are based on strict, well-defined customs. One of the most sensitive and important of these customs involves the use of introductions when calling on someone for either social or business purposes.

The Japanese generally do not expect foreigners to follow their etiquette, and regularly make exceptions on behalf of visitors, but this is one area where the visitor should definitely make an effort to "do as the Japanese do."

The difference an introduction makes in the reception one gets, regardless of the purpose, is really remarkable because the *shokaijo* (show-kie-joe) introduction system is so deeply ingrained in the Japanese that they may not react freely if it is not followed.

Ideally, an introduction is from a friend or associate of the person you want to meet and, of course, one that is held in high esteem by him. If such an individual is not available, an introduction from a well-known bank or company is second best.

Getting Around the Maze

Finding an address in Japan is very much like finding the proverbial needle in a haystack. In the first place, addresses of buildings or homes have no relation to any street they may be on or near. In the second place, only a small percentage of the streets in Japanese cities have names.

Addresses are related to areas rather than streets. The areas start out with the city (Tokyo) and go from *ku* (wards) to *cho* (which orginally meant "town" but is better translated as "section"), and finally to *banchi* (or lots). This smallest area, banchi, usually has three or four and may have dozens of buildings or homes on it—some with the same address.

A typical address, written in the proper order, goes like this: Tokyo, Shibuya-ku, 7 Nishi-cho, 15-3 banchi, Suzuki Kinya, Mr.

The problem is made more complex by the fact that both the streets and the dimensions of the areas are irregular in size and shape, and no obvious way exists to tell where one area ends and another begins.

The problem may not be so difficult if you are going to a well-known building or site, and if you happen to get a taxi driver who has been driving in the city long enough to be familiar with such places. Unfortunately, there is such a turnover among taxi drivers that it is not at all odd to get one who doesn't even know the location of Tokyo Central Station.

The wisest thing to do, regardless of where you are going, is to have your destination written out in Japanese on a card or slip of paper (by your hotel clerk, maid, bellboy, etc.) so you can show it to a taxi driver, a policeman or—in a dire emergency—to a passerby. And this holds true even if you are going to such landmarks as the Takashimaya Department Store, because the average visitor cannot pronounce Takashimaya (tah-cah-she-mah-yah) well enough for the average taxi driver to understand it.

If you are going to an out-of-the way restaurant or shop, or to an "unknown" place right in the heart of town, it is essential to know exactly where the place is in relation to something that is known—which means that you almost have to have a hand-drawn map showing this relationship.

Many Japanese places of business provide name cards that include maps of their location. All Japanese, but especially hotel clerks, have had considerable experience at drawing maps for themselves as well as others.

If you should want to go to a location that is not known to whoever is helping you, ask your helper to telephone the place and get specific details about where it is, and how to get there by cab or whatever means of transportation you are going to use.

Seriously, a regular pathfinder—born and raised in Tokyo and blessed with ESP—must go through all of the steps above each time he goes to a new place, if he wants to avoid wasting a great deal of time and possibly money. So, prepare yourself.

There are small police "boxes" (*koban*) every

few blocks in Japanese cities, all manned by one or more policemen whose main occupation consists of giving directions to people. Some of the officers speak a little English. If they do not, they will customarily call in someone who does when the need arises.

Each of the *koban* is equipped with detailed maps of the surrounding area for the officers to refer to if they cannot answer an inquiry offhand.

Another source of directions sometimes superior to that provided by the koban police is noodle delivery boys. They can usually pinpoint every house or building within a several-block radius.

Those "Notorious" Taxis

Japan's taxi drivers have a rather unsavory reputation but actually most of it is underserved —or rather the reputation certainly does *not* apply to the majority of the drivers. All things considered, the taxis and their drivers are invaluable to hundreds of thousands of people every day—especially to visitors from abroad, who would be practically immobilized without them.

Every hotel of any importance in Japan has a regular "taxi stand" at the main entrance, and when the supply of waiting taxis runs out, the doormen go into the streets and flag down cruising cabs.

At major hotels, doormen also supervise the loading and unloading of taxis, and double as interpreters for foreign passengers.

Since driving in Japan is on the left side of the street, passengers enter and leave cabs through the door on the left side. In virtually all cabs, this door is opened and closed electrically by the taxi driver, so first of all do not attempt to open the door manually; second, step slightly to the rear of the door when you approach the cab so the opening door won't bang into you.

There are two categories of cabs: those that are company-owned, and those that are owned by the driver. The latter cabs are marked by two large ideograms on the doors that are read *kojin* and can be translated as "privately owned." The owners of these cabs have had at least 10 years' driving experience, and as a rule are the safest and most knowledgeable drivers.

While it is against the law for a taxi driver to refuse a passenger when his cab is vacant, it nevertheless happens, especially late at night in entertainment districts and when it is raining. On these occasions, the drivers know they can find passengers who will pay them several times the meter reading (which they signal by holding up two, three or more fingers).

These drivers also like to pick up groups of people because (if they are Japanese) they will likely be going to different destinations. Some taxis simply drive on by foreigners as well as Japanese who do not give the "right" signal.

Taxi drivers are not tipped except under unusual circumstances, such as when they help the passenger load and unload several bags, or spend an inordinate amount of time asking directions at police boxes, etc., in an effort to pinpoint a hard-to-find destination for a passenger.

How to Call a Clerk

Visitors to *Nihon* who do not speak the language and are not familiar with the non-verbal communication signals are often at a loss when it comes to getting help in a store or office.

Unlike Western places of business, the Japanese may not immediately descend upon a visitor or customer to inquire about what he wants, particularly in department stores, shops or offices that are not regularly patronized by Westerners. In the traditional Japanese system, it is regarded as impolite to aggressively approach a customer or visitor without any sign from him.

Clerks frequently *do not* respond to a questioning look or any other facial expression that in the West would get the desired reaction.

In Japan there are two accepted ways to call people to you non-verbally. The first one is by waving your hand at them. Hold your hand up in front of you, palm down, and wave it up and down, very much like one waves goodby in the West. Remember, however, that this signal is *not* to be used to an older person in a non-service position or to one of rank or authority. It should be used *only* to young clerks, maids, waiters, workmen, children, and so on.

The other method, which may be used to anyone but is normally used in more formal situations and to people toward whom a certain respect is expected, is simply to catch the eye of the other party, dip your head in a quick, shallow bow, and look at him or her expectantly until he comes forward or sends someone else to see what you want.

In days past, it was common for men at drinking parties and traditionally styled restaurants to call waitresses and maids by clapping their hands loudly. While still in use, particularly by older men, this custom is no longer considered "good manners" and is not recommended.

If you try the bow-approach to a young person in a place of business and get no reaction, combine it with a short hand-wave. Quite frequently, people in places where Western visitors are uncommon will hold back because they assume they will not be able to communicate with you.

Since the non-verbal signals described here are "in Japanese," using them helps, at least initially, to break the language and cultural barrier and put the person at ease. If you think you might get into a situation where the Japanese you approach cannot reasonably be expected to speak English, you should prepare for the eventuality by having the purpose of your visit written out; or be ready to use some other such ploy.

Another hand-signal that very often comes in handy (!) is one that means "no," and is most often used when someone asks you if you want something. Just wave your right hand back-and-forth in front of your nose, holding it so the palm is pointed to the left.

Checking Into an Inn

It usually (and hopefully) isn't very long before the typical visitor to Japan finds him or herself in a *ryokan* (rio-khan) or inn. I happened to be convinced that the Japanese inn is one of the most excellent institutions ever developed, and hope that a few insights into the character and personality of ordinary ryokan will help you enjoy them as much as I do.

First, the inn is not a hotel and should not be confused with one. It is basically a villa-like home that has extra rooms and takes in guests. The exterior of the inn is designed to complement and merge in with nature, and is set in a garden or amidst spectacular natural scenery such as a mountain, valley or gorge—and as often as possible is on the bank of a river or swift-flowing mountain stream.

The interior of the inn is designed to function as and give the feeling of a large summer or resort-type home in which all the patrons are honored guests. Each room has its own *tokonoma* (toe-coe-no-mah) beauty alcove, and usually a *lanai* that overlooks nature outside.

Inns are not designed to provide tight privacy, but to encourage the guest to relax, expand and communicate with his surroundings. This relaxation process begins at the doorway, when you remove your shoes and put on hallway slippers.

These slippers are worn on areas where there is wood, stone, or tile. They are not worn into rooms that have *tatami* (tah-tah-me) reedmat floors, but are left in the hallway outside your room or in the *genkan* (gang-khan) vestibule of the room.

Your room will be furnished with a low table and probably a low dresser/mirror. It may have an adjoining sitting room with Western-style lounge chairs, and there are often chairs on the *lanai*. Your maids, assigned to you as soon as you check in, will take *zabuton* (zah-boo-tone) sitting cushions from wall closets and put them on the floor for you.

As soon as you are shown into your room you are usually offered tea and usually tiny cakes. At the same time, if not before, you will also be offered a *yukata* robe. Men often just remove their jackets.

After a brief period of refreshing yourself, the usual procedure after checking into an inn is to take a bath, but if you arrive early in the day this may be postponed until evening.

The traditional inn has no dining room. Guests are served individually in their own rooms by maids, who may be summoned at any time by an electric call-button. (The rates usually include breakfast and dinner.) The typical inn does not have a bar, but in addition to eating in your room, you can order drinks delivered to you wherever you might be in the inn or on the grounds. Inns are at their best during warm months.

Some ryokan have refrigerators in their rooms that are well-stocked with beer and various snack items. Guests take whatever they want from the fridges, keeping record of what they eat or drink on a form provided for that purpose. The total is added to your bill.

Note: check-out time in ryokan is usually 10 a.m. Most inns also close and lock their front doors at set times in the evening; some as early as 10 p.m. If you are staying at an inn, be sure you know what time the front door is locked, and if necessary make arrangements to be let in at a later hour.

You and Your *Yukata*

Most visitors who treat themselves to the special pleasures of the Japanese inn are quick to recognize the extraordinary contribution the *yukata* makes to the attractions of living Japanese style.

The *yukata* began as an undergarment for the kimono, and later was used as a nightgown and a bathrobe. Then, decorations were added to the thin cotton robe and it gradually developed into an outer garment as well. Long before the beginning of the modern era, the *yukata* had become the national leisure costume of Japan.

The *yukata* owes much of its special appeal to the fact that it is still a combination bedroom, bath and outside leisure garment, and to the intimacy of the *ryokan* and the resort, especially during the warm summer months when it may be worn without undergarments.

Also, the nature of the *yukata* hugging the body from neck to ankle, makes it necessary for the wearer to move in a relatively slow, controlled manner, thereby contributing to a quality of gracefulness and physical discipline that is pleasing to the eye and the spirit.

The patterns and cuts of the *yukata* are different for men and women, but it takes a bit of exposure before the unfamiliar eye automatically discerns the difference. *Yukata* that are designed primarily as sleeping gowns have sleeves that are extra long.

There are a number of considerations to keep in mind regarding the *yukata*. Probably the most common "mistake" foreign visitors make when first introduced to the multi-purpose robe is "lapping" the front right-over-left instead of left-over-right. The former is symbolic of death.

There is also a right way and a wrong way for the *yukata* sash to be tied. Men wrap the sash low around their hips, with the knot on the right side. Women wrap the sash (or *obi*) high, and tie it in back.

During the winter months, a padded version of the *yukata* called a *tanzen* (tahnzen) is provided by inns. Summer is of course the best season for *yukata*, when you will find that the clean, crisply starched, colorful garment will add another dimension to your stay in Japan.

Hot Bath Behavior

The most distinctive feature of the Japanese *O'furo* (Oh-foo-row) hot bath is that you bathe before getting into the tub or pool. The baths, both public and private, are designed in such a way that you soap up and wash off outside on tiled or board floors that are slanted and have run-off drains.

Temperatures in the *O'furo* vary from 95 degrees F. to as high as 140 degrees F., and unless you are in a private bath it is not cricket to put cold water into the tub just to suit yourself.

All Japanese inns have traditionally styled baths, and a number of the new Western hotels now offer *O'furo* facilities with some suites, or separate as "Turkish baths." Soap and towels are provided except at public baths. In inns the towel is usually a very thin cotton cloth called *tenugui* (tay-new-gooey), which is used as a washcloth and drying towel.

Most inns that cater to foreign visitors have two types of baths. A small one for singles, couples, and families, sometimes known as a *kazoku-buro* (cah-zoe-coo booh-row) or "family bath"; and a larger one—usually co-educational—for groups. Very large inns may have several baths of different sizes.

The routine is very simple. You may undress in your room and wear a *yukata* to the bath, or wear your clothing to the bath "ante-room" and undress there. Whatever you wear to the ante-room is left there in a wicker basket or a shelf niche provided for that purpose.

After undressing, you pass through a sliding door into the main area of the bath. Depending on the size of the bath, there will be anywhere from one to dozens of hot-and-cold water spigot combinations along one or more sides.

Select one of the water outlets, either squat in front of it or sit on a tiny wooden bench-stool usually available, proceed to douse yourself with water, and scrub. After washing and rinsing yourself thoroughly, enter the bath and soak for as long as you wish.

It will soon be obvious that the cooler water is at the bottom of the pool, and that any movement increases the burning effects of the water.

After a period in the tub, the usual procedure, especially for those who stay in the bath a long time, is to douse one's self with several buckets of cool or cold water. Then you wipe and sponge off most of the water with your wet *tenugui*, return to the ante-room where you finish drying, and put on *yukata* or your own clothing, depending on what you intend to do afterward.

In most private-home baths and baths in some smaller inns there are no wall spigots for hot water, and the hot water to be used for dousing and scrubbing is drawn from the tub by means of a small wooden bucket, a large dipper, or very often a washpan.

Although the routine described above is the proper one, it is very common for men, especially in public bathhouses, to breach etiquette in the wintertime when it is cold. Instead of scrubbing first, they will enter the tub first to warm up. Then they get out and wash, and later get back in the tub a second time to soak.

Of course, this results in the water getting much dirtier sooner, but even after several dozen unwashed persons have soaked in a large tub for a few minutes, the water at least looks cleaner than if just one person soaps-up and scrubs in a small American-style tub.

As has also been widely publicized, the Japanese do not regard mixed-bathing as scandalous, extraordinary, or even exciting. And I am happy to report that more and more Westerners are discovering that mixed-bathing has very special therapeutic effects contributing to a more stable personality.

If you have the opportunity and inclination to group-bathe—and I highly recommend the custom—the only additional etiquette involved is to very nonchalantly cover yourself with your *tenugui* towel when you enter and leave the bath, and when walking around inside the bathroom. Not everyone bothers to do this but it is considered polite.

Of course, it would be considered scandalous for anyone to make any kind of fuss over being nude or seeing others nude in a bath.

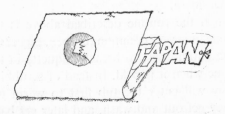

You and Miss Turkish Bath

The *geisha* and *maiko* are a lot more romantic and better known, but Japan's Turkish-bath girls contribute a great deal more to the success of the country as the world's best travel-vacation area.

For the uninitiated, a Turkish bath is a kind of bath in which the bather, after a period of heavy perspiration in a steam or heat "cabinet," is washed, massaged, and cooled by one or more persons skilled in this line of work.

What makes Japan's Turkish baths unusual and interesting, particularly to men, is that these various ministrations are performed by attractive young girls usually dressed in shorts and halters.

Turkish baths have been popular in Japan for several centuries—at one time they virtually replaced the formerly great redlight districts as houses of sensual pleasure—and there are several hundreds of them in the largest cities today.

Many of the *"Toruko"* are very ornate, some are luxurious, and a few are gigantic in size. The largest one in the country at this writing is the *New Japan* in Osaka. It has eight stories above the ground and two below, and includes one floor that caters exclusively to women. Facilities and service vary to some extent, but most Turkish bathhouses serve drinks to order, and some include restaurants. Room service for at least drinks is a common feature.

The typical bath is set up something like a hotel, with a reception desk and a waiting lobby that may or may not have semi-private sections. The customer may call in for an appointment at a specific time, or just walk in and take his turn. Those who have patronized a place before often request a certain girl.

At the appointed time, or when the walk-in customer's turn comes, the lucky girl comes to the lobby and escorts the patron to a private bath-suite. Besides the steam-cabinet and bath, the room will include a massage table, a place for the guest to hang his clothes, a dressing mirror, and perhaps a chair.

The guest removes his shoes before stepping up on the floor of the room. The girl helps him strip, hands him a towel to wrap around his waist, then takes him to the steam cabinet. While he is in the "box," she checks the bath, occasionally wipes the sweat from his brow, and if he has ordered a drink, holds it up to his mouth when he wants a sip.

When the bather indicates that he is "well-done," the girl lets him out of the box, takes the towel from his waist, douses him with a few buckets of warm water, and has him get into the tub and soak for a few minutes. Then he gets out and sits on a low bench-stool while the girl scrubs him all over—or mostly all over, depending upon her inclinations.

After the hard scrubbing, the girl douses the guest with more buckets of water. He may then get back in the tub for a few minutes before he is dried off and directed to the massage bunk.

Most girls will ask you to lay face down first, covering your mid section with another towel. After thoroughly massaging your back from neck to toes (she will get up and walk on your back if you like), she turns you over and does the front.

While the Turkish baths are mostly patronized by men, some of them welcome female guests and a surprisingly large number of lady visitors take advantage of them. I have letters in my files from women who say that the Turkish bathhouses were a major highlight of their trip.

One of the special services provided by most of the baths is washing the guest's underclothing. The items are returned to the rooms, heat-dried and pressed, before the guest is done. Other special services include several "kinds" of baths, ranging from milk and lemon to aphrodisiac baths.

The Turkish bathhouses have a reputation that is salacious to say the least. Whether or not this reputation is deserved, the baths do not disappoint many people.

In a Japanese *Benjo* (Toilet)

There are several words for "toilet" in Japanese. Women usually use *gofujo* (go-foo-joe), which means the "honorable motion place." Or they might use *O'toire* (Oh-toy-ray) which is simply a Japanese pronunciation of toilet. Both men and women frequently use the word *O'tearai* (Oh-tay-ah-rye) or "place for washing hands." Men in informal situations will most often use the more colloquial *benjo* (bane-joe), which literally means "convenient place."

The Japanese *benjo* deserves some comment, since you are likely to encounter it in most inns, in some private homes you may visit, in traditionally styled restaurants, in mountain-climber huts, and so on.

Basically, the *benjo* consists of either (1) an aperture over a pit in the ground; (2) a ceramic flush bowl over a pit; or (3) a ceramic flush bowl connected to plumbing. The first type is the most primitive, and the last type is the most modern. The one common feature that all of the types share is that the user squats over the aperture or the flush bowl.

In case the reader is not aware of it, Western medical and health authorities are unanimous in saying that the natural and most desirable position for using a toilet is the squat. Of course, this is no particular help to a person who is many pounds overweight and in some cases hasn't squatted in 30 years or more. Since many people are in this category, it behooves them to find out if they really can squat before visiting a place that has only *benjo* facilities.

Most public places—inns, restaurants, bars—have flush-type toilets, but the non-flush type are still common in private homes, particularly away from the great metropolitan areas. Hotels and public buildings have Western-type commodes and urinals.

Japanese *benjo*, especially in small apartment buildings and in some restaurants and bars, are very small—so small, in fact, that a large person may have difficulty in getting down and up in them. One can squat down in a smaller space than he can get up in, and if you find yourself in this position, the only solution is to waddle out into the hallway and stand up there.

At inns, guests wear felt or plastic slippers when walking around in the hallways and lobbies, but the same slippers are never worn into the toilet. Separate "toilet slippers"—often made of heavy straw—are provided for wearing inside toilets. You leave your regular slippers outside.

Many public toilets in Japan and those at many restaurants and night spots are co-educational, so don't be surprised or upset if a member of the opposite sex trots in to join you—or is already ensconced when you enter. Just act like it's old hat, and enjoy yourself.

Take special note that toilets on trains, except for those on the "Green Cars" of the famous "Bullet Trains," are squat-style. Women wearing high heels may want to remove them before using squat train toilets because the motion of the train plus heels may present problems.

If you are going to be out of your hotel or inn

a great deal, it is wise to carry toilet paper with you in your purse or pocket, because it often happens that public toilets have run out.

Commuter Train Tactics

Japan's commuter trains and subways are internationally reknowned for being on time and efficient—most run every 2 to 4 minutes. They are also famous for being unbelievably crowded during rush-hours—up to 400 percent of "normal capacity."

This *kotsu jigoku* (coat-sue gee-go-coo) or "transportation hell" as the Japanese call it, regularly causes injury to body and limb, not to mention clothing.

Commuters are very good at lining up at individual coach stops along the platform—in subway stations the places to stand are clearly marked on the platforms. But once the interchange of passengers begins it is more or less every man for himself.

The first thing to beware of is standing directly in front of a door when it opens to discharge passengers. You must move aside quickly to avoid being pushed aside, or run down.

When boarding a very crowded train, on which standing passengers are really packed in as tight as un-oiled sardines, try to avoid being caught in the middle of the aisle where you cannot reach a hand-strap or side-bar to hold onto. There is too much danger of going down with the whole crowd when the train starts, stops or sways.

In this position you are also likely to be buffeted first one way then the other, each time passengers embark or disembark. The best idea is to wedge yourself into a corner or niche formed by the seats and sides of the coach, next to the doors.

This way you will be able to grasp either an overhead strap or hand-bar, and you will also be able to see out of the car and check the names of the stations before the car comes to a halt.

Any woman who rides commuter trains during rush-hours is advised to avoid wearing high heels, to keep her purse in front of her, clutched to her chest, and not to wear fragile clothing.

The main weekday rush-hours are from about 7:00 to 9:30 and from around 4:30 to 7:00. On holidays and summer weekends, trains going to beach and mountain-resort areas are generally packed beyond "capacity," and it is customary for vacationers to form lines several hours in advance of departure times.

Summer mountain climbers and winter skiers literally "camp out" by the thousands at such stations as Shinjuku and Ueno in Tokyo during the height of these two seasons, sometimes spending as much as half a day and a full night on the platforms.

If you choose to ride the commuter or vacation trains, try to do your traveling during off-hours. If you plan on taking resort trains during the busiest seasons—and they can be fun with a group—get your tickets as early as possible, with reserved seats if they are available.

Train and subway stations everywhere in Japan except a few rural areas generally have the names of the stations in Romanized Japanese (which amounts to "English") as well as in the native ideograms (*kanji*). This, of course, is a tremendous boon for the non-Japanese-reading visitor.

Furthermore, most signs, which are repeated several times in each station, include the names of the stations just before and just after—so you know in advance what the next station is going to be. The before-and-after stations are at the bottom of the signs, in smaller letters.

Getting to the Trains on Time

It is quite an experience to ride cross-country trains in Japan, particularly, of course, the famous "bullet" trains that travel between Tokyo, Nagoya, Kyoto, Osaka, and Okayama at well over 100 miles an hour.

Traveling by train in Japan can be complicated, however, because of the size of the stations, the number of trains coming and going every few seconds and minutes, the great crowds of people embarking and disembarking, the difficulty in identifying coaches, the foreign language, etc.

To minimize these difficulties it is wise if not essential that you buy your tickets as early as possible through a travel service; allow yourself plenty of extra time to get to the station, find the right platform and the right boarding spot; and make sure that you have all the details concerning the trip written down.

Ideally, you will have a member of the travel service accompany you to the station to make sure that you get on the right train at the right time.

Seating Etiquette

Some Western visitors in Japan may be irritated by the seating etiquette of the Japanese aboard crowded commuter trains and other public transportation. Partly because the "ladies first" custom is not common except where very old persons and mothers with young children are concerned, but mostly because of their treatment of children.

Young mothers habitually stand so that their children can sit or stand on the seat and look out the window. Even old people, particularly old women, will frequently get up and let robust and rowdy young boys and girls have their seats. There are practical reasons for this, however, since smaller children could easily get hurt standing up on crowded trains.

On trains and in theaters the Japanese "save" seats by putting or leaving something in them. This custom is of course practiced in the West, but in Japan it sometimes goes a little further. If some travelers or theater-goers can get something into a particular seat before actually taking physical possession of it, they regard it as "saved."

When one gets up and leaves a seat, it is customary to leave something in it to show that it is occupied.

Driving is Deadly Serious

Driving is a more serious business in Japan than in most Western countries, for several reasons. Many of the streets and roadways are inadequate as automobile thoroughfares. The streets, roads, and highways that do exist are often incredibly crowded. The narrower the street the less likely it is to have sidewalks, and the more likely it is to double as a walkway for pedestrians (somewhere around 80 percent of all the streets in the country fit this category).

In addition, many of Japan's drivers have had relatively little experience in driving, having obtained their first car only recently. Japanese pedestrians are not car-danger-conscious the way Americans are; plus they tend to assume that they have just as much right in the streets as cars, since they have to walk somewhere.

For the visitor who cannot read street and highway signs, does not know the streets and highways, and has never driven under such adverse conditions, driving in Japan is of course an even more serious proposition than it is for the Japanese.

Driving in Japan is on the left side. Right-of-way is legally the same as in the U.S., but in practice it is quite different. You cannot assume that the other driver will obey traffic regulations or extend "road courtesy." You must watch out for yourself.

Professional drivers, such as truck drivers and the wilder taxi drivers, appear to concern themselves only about the space immediately in front of their vehicles, and as long as that is clear they tend to barrel ahead without regard for what may be going on beside or behind them.

You *can* drive in Japan—even in Tokyo or one of the other major cities—but you must be prepared to contend with all the factors mentioned above, plus a few less obvious ones.

A vast highway improvement program has been under way in Japan for several years, and there are now excellent freeways linking many cities and places of interest. There is no more delightful way to visit Hakone or famous places along the beautiful Izu Peninsula than by private automobile.

If you decide to drive, you can save yourself a great deal of uncertainty and possible frustration by inviting a Japanese friend to accompany you to serve as a sign-reader, interpreter and general life-saver.

The ideal situation, if you want to travel by private car in Japan and can afford it, is to hire a driver, available through the various hire or rent-a-car systems.

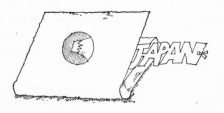

Telling a Shrine from a Temple

There are over 100,000 shrines in Japan, and many thousands of temples. Shrines, of course, are Shintoist and temples are Buddhist.

Shrines are marked by one or more of the famous *torii* (toe-reee) gates, consisting of two upright pillars and one or two cross pieces at the top. Shrines are usually small, austere structures. Shinto priests wear white robes, and female attendants wear white blouses and scarlet skirts.

Worshippers do not enter shrines, but pay their respects outside, standing before the shrine altar. Shinto has no sacred literature, but it does have colorful ceremonies on festive and other auspicious occasions.

Buddhist temples, on the other hand, are often great and remarkable edifices, and are the repositories of a vast literature and works of art in many fields. Some of the great Buddhist monasteries include many temples in one complex. Buddhists enter their temples to worship. Priests wear black robes.

Among the best-known and most impressive shrines in Tokyo are the Yasukuni and the Meiji. The Heian is one of the most popular of the dozens of shrines in Kyoto, and the most famous of all of Japan's shrines is the Grand Shrine of Ise, near Nagoya, where emperors are enthroned and where the spirits of past emperors are enshrined.

Noted temples in Tokyo include the Zojoji, the Sengakuji and the Asakusa Kannon. Dozens of temples in Kyoto have been nationally famous for centuries. Among them: Chion-in, Kinkakuji (The Temple of the Golden Pavilion), Kiyomizu, Nansenji, Higashi Honganji, Ryoanji, Daitokuji, and so on.

Stretching Your Yen at Night

Japan probably has more nightlife than any other country, with giant entertainment districts a distinct and colorful feature of every city. In Tokyo alone over one-half million women, including some 150,000 cabaret hostesses, are employed in the entertainment business. But fun in this exotic "floating world" can be very expensive, especially for the newcomer who is not familiar with the scene.

Probably the most important thing to keep in mind is that all first-class restaurants, bars, and clubs can be expected to charge prices on a par with or higher than comparable places in New York.

A second point to keep in mind where bars and clubs are concerned, is that the Japanese practice of providing guests with the company of attractive female companions entails an expense over and above what you would spend in a New York night spot.

A third point is that exclusive Japanese-styled restaurants and "private-club-like" bars are patronized primarily by men on liberal entertainment expense accounts. These places customarily charge what they judge the "traffic" will bear, and do not necessarily relate the size of the bill to how much liquor was consumed, how much food was eaten, or how many hostesses or geisha were involved.

When a casual customer wanders into one of these places on his own and without an introduction (something only a green foreigner would normally do), he will very likely be charged at the same rate that the bar applies to its expense account clientele—and he may end up with a bill five to 10 times higher than he expected.

The only way to go to these places, unless you are a genuine "Big Spender," is as the guest of Japanese or foreign friends who know what they are doing and can afford the expense.

Fortunately, there are more than enough "non-exclusive" places that do cater to visitors from abroad, and have menus and set prices so that you can judge about what your bill is going to be.

There are several types of night sports in Japan, and the variations can be confusing. Generally speaking, however, we can categorize them as clubs, cabarets, bars and beer halls.

The so-called night club serves food, has live entertainment, and features patron dancing. Night clubs cater to singles and couples, and if a customer wants a hostess to be his companion for the evening, he asks for one. At some clubs, if he sits at a table instead of the bar it is more or less taken for granted that he wants a hostess. The girls are charged for by the hour.

Cabarets vary in size, but are often gigantic, and very elaborate. Some of them serve food; others do not. Most have live entertainment. They cater to men only and every guest who comes in is expected to take a girl. If he doesn't request a specific girl, one is assigned to him. A customer in a cabaret can refuse to accept a girl, but he will not be popular. There is patron dancing, and the customer pays for his companion by the hour.

This brings us to the two basic types of bars, one that has hostesses and one that does not. Actually, to employ hostesses a place must be registered as a cabaret, but many smaller, less pretentious places prefer to call themselves bars. In bars with hostesses, it is taken for granted that every customer wants a girl to join him, but there is no special fuss if a customer wants to sit and drink alone.

In most such hostess-bars, a girl will automatically attach herself to each customer who comes in (if there are free girls) but she will not stay with him long unless he buys her drinks or is a big drinker himself, because her income is based on how much the customer spends on drinks.

In some cases, a place that looks and acts like a bar will charge for its girls by the hour, or will use a combination system of time rates and "hostess drinks" to pay its girls. In places where the girls are assigned to customers automatically, the customer can ask for a different girl if he doesn't like the one he got. But this doesn't make him popular with the girls.

In smaller, more exclusive cabarets where every customer is expected to take a girl, the unwary guest occasionally finds himself presented with a bill of astronomical size, without knowing why. This is a system that might be called "musical chairs." On slow nights, several girls may take turns and each one will spend a few minutes at a customer's table. The idea is that the customer is expected to pay a minimum hour's fee for every girl who favors him with her company.

This practice is not necessarily malicious. The girls and clubs do it regularly to Japanese customers, who of course know about it and can object if they want to. Many who are on large expense accounts, or are financially well off, often encourage this kind of treatment because it gives them status in the entertainment world—and, of course, the various services the girls provide generally improve in proportion to the patron's generosity.

Closing time for night spots in Japan, unless they are licensed as restaurants, is 11:30. The peak hours are from about 8:00 to 11:00. A 10-percent entertainment tax is added to all bills over 600 yen.

There are, however, quite a few night spots that stay open, clandestinely, after the official closing time. These places darken their windows and doors to avoid attracting the attention of patrolling police. They also station lookouts near buzzers at the entrance in case the police decide to make a spot check.

If the alarm is sounded, patrons who are dancing rush back to their tables and sit down, and the members of the band (if there is a band) grab their musical instruments and dash for a backroom or the toilet.

Girls Are Not Taboo, But . . .

It is common knowledge that Western men find Oriental girls unusually attractive, and few if any Asian girls are as attractive as the Japanese. Japanese girls are also attracted to Western men. This combination can cause problems for the visiting male if he is not aware of some of the etiquette involved.

The Japanese do not mind it when visiting foreign men enjoy themselves with Japanese girls. In fact, they encourage it—but *only* with girls who are in the business of entertainment: night club hostesses, Turkish bath girls, etc.

Furthermore, the rules of the game ideally limit these associations to the girls' places of business or to certain types of places where discreet assignations are the order of business.

It goes without saying that few if any foreigners, visiting or resident, consciously follow these unwritten rules except when it serves their own private purposes.

Probably the most common faux pas pulled by Western men visiting Japan is taking young ladies of the evening (so to speak) to popular public places where they mix with the elite of society. At best, these men appear to be lacking in refinement.

At the same time, the newly arrived man in Japan should not be surprised when the beautiful, provocative-acting cabaret hostess who readily agrees to meet him for a late-night date after closing time fails to show up at the appointed place. She is sought after by many men

every night, and the "I'll meet you on the corner" routine is one of the standard ploys she
uses to fend off would-be lotharios. Girls who
really intend to keep after-work dates with
cabaret patrons will usually agree to leave the
club with them at closing time.

A male guest in a Japanese inn should also
not assume that a maid is available as a pillow
partner just because she helps him remove his
clothing and don a *yukata* and/or keeps popping
in and out of his room while he is in bed or
undressed.

It would be foolish to state that the maids who
do this as part of their job are completely oblivi-
ous to the masculinity of their guests, but the
code of conduct followed by the average *ryokan*
maid does not permit her to engage in "instant
romances" with guests.

She will, however, engage in stimulating
banter without reserve, and will often tease a
guest with artful coquetry. But this is usually as
far as the game goes.

Getting acquainted with and dating Japanese
girls who are not employed in the entertainment
trades follows the same general pattern as in the
U.S., except that as a rule, males at this point do
not pick up their dates at home or return them
there.

How to Drink & Stay Sober

Drinking alcoholic beverages is an integral and important part of interpersonal relations in Japan. There are both social and business occasions when drinking is expected of everyone who is physically able, although many women do so only in token amounts.

The traveler in Japan fairly often finds himself in a situation where he is expected to drink enthusiastically. The most common occasion is at a large Japanese-style dinner when, among other things, every person may be expected to drink a toast with every other person at the party.

This can present a real challenge, even when the drinking implement is the tiny, thimble-sized *sakazuki* from which *O'sake* is imbibed.

If you do not drink, about the only acceptable excuse is that you have a stomach ailment and are under doctors orders to avoid all alcohol (older women are not under such pressure to drink, but younger ones often cannot escape).

A very good gambit that you can use to avoid drinking more than you want is to act like you are much drunker than you are. As soon as you show exaggerated signs of inebriation you are not expected to drink any more.

When you have had all you want, turn your cup or glass upside down and politely but firmly resist all entreaties to reverse it. If you are not a strong drinker, it is wise to eat something that will line your stomach before going to a banquet-party.

It is good manners to pick up and hold your

glass or cup while it is being filled, and it is also proper etiquette for you to take at least a sip before setting it down. At such parties, it is good form to go to the host's table and pour him a drink. He will pour one for you in turn. If your host or anyone else at the party pours a drink for you, it is proper and expected for you to return the gesture. Good friends will drink out of each other's cups. At formal parties, bowls of hot water are provided for rinsing cups before passing them around.

Many Japanese are very strong drinkers. It is not a good idea to try to outdrink them just to "save face." Japan's traditional drinking toast is *kampai*! (kahm-pie), which means something like "bottom's up." You will hear it often.

When the Earth Quakes

There are several thousand recordable earthquakes a year in Japan. Generally, during the course of a year, there will be from three to a dozen that will be severe enough to rattle furnishings and otherwise attract attention to themselves. About once a year, a quake is bad enough that it will cause damage somewhere near the epicenter.

The visitor to Japan is not likely to experience a bad earthquake because they are not that frequent and the center is usually some distance away from main cities.

The Japanese have made great improvements in earthquake-proof construction techniques in recent years, so that large areas of major cities are now safe from any ordinary quake.

Most quakes are over before you can take any action. Others may last for several minutes. If you are in a large concrete and steel building the best thing to do is stay where you are. If it really gets bad, turn off any gas that may be on, open the door and get under something—or stand in the doorway. If you are in your hotel room or a private home, turn on the water faucets to catch as much water as you can (in case the water mains break), if you have time to do so before taking cover. If you are in a small wooden building and the quake is obviously a serious one, get to the outside doorway so you can run outside if necessary. If you are in the street, run inside the doorway of the nearest large building.

In a Japanese Home

The Japanese do not ordinarily invite strangers, casual acquaintances, or business associates into their homes the way Americans do. But it is not so uncommon for them to invite foreign guests, especially travelers, into their homes.

Nowadays, many affluent urban Japanese live in homes or apartments that are mostly Western in construction and furnishings, and no etiquette beyond ordinary courtesy is required to behave properly enough in such residences.

The majority of Japanese, however, still live in homes that would be described as "Japanese style" because they have *tatami* (reed mat) floors, sliding paper wall panels and inner doors. These homes have only a minimum of furniture. The family sits on floor cushions (*zabuton*) and sleeps on thick floor mats kept in closets when not being used (or aired out).

The most important things to keep in mind here is to take your shoes off at the entrance-way, sit where your host suggests, and at least try whatever refreshments are offered to you. Other than this, ordinary courtesy again will more than suffice.

Climate & Clothing

The climate in Japan is often described as "temperate," which can be confusing. The Japanese islands lie mostly in the North Temperate Zone, and stretch some 2,600 kilometers (1,600 miles) from north to south.

The adjoining land-mass of Siberia, Korea and Manchuria to the northwest, along with the ridge of high mountains running, spine-like, north-to-south through Japan, also play a vital role in the climate—which is general terms resembles that of the Eastern Seaboard of the U.S. from Bangor, Maine down to Jacksonville, Florida.

Mean winter temperature in Tokyo is 38.7 degrees F., and humidity averages 60 percent. In spring, the mean temperature is 55.6 degrees F, with humidity averaging 68 percent. Summertime temperatures in Tokyo range from 75 to 85, with mean humidity 80. It cools off in the fall to a mean 62.1 degrees F, with humidity averaging 77 percent. Temperatures in Kyoto are a little lower in winter and a little higher in summer than those in Tokyo.

As for clothing, it should be very warm but not heavy in winter, unless you are going to northern Japan or to the mountains; light but warm in spring; very light in summer, and again light but warm in the fall. If you are going to mountainous areas or the far north in the spring or fall, warm clothing is very important, especially at night and on overcast, cloudy days.

There are monsoon-type spring and late fall

rainy seasons throughout Japan, but it can rain, particularly in mountain areas, anytime. A light raincoat is very useful. Formal clothing is not needed in Japan except for special occasions. Men wear jackets and ties in better clubs and dining places, especially in the evening. Otherwise, dress for both men and women is casual.

Things Travelers Fail to Do

Almost every person who visits Japan finds, after he has returned home, that there are several things he failed to do which he very much regrets. To avoid finding yourself in this category:

Keep a good, clearly written address-book to list all of the names and addresses of people you may want to contact later or recommend to friends.

Obtain the names and addresses of shops that sell by mail order so that you can later send for the things you missed, didn't have room for, or couldn't afford.

Buy at least two art or handicraft items of real quality and merit to keep permanently as tangible reminders of your trip.

Take all of the pictures you should have.

Buy a cookbook so that you can add at least one or two of your favorite Japanese dishes to your culinary repertoire.

Stay in a Japanese inn and visit a Turkish bathhouse.

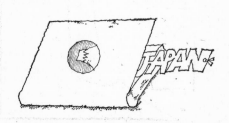

Is It Safe to Eat & Drink?

By all means! The "Tourist Trot," or whatever the bug is called in other countries, is virtually unknown in Japan. All water in Japanese cities and resorts is purified by the most modern methods, and chemical fertilizers are used on vegetables served in hotels.

In 15 years of living and traveling in Japan, I have never experienced *La Turista*, and have been aware of only one genuine case.

Those 3-Minute Telephones

Japan is well supplied with public telephones. They are painted a bright red, and can be found almost everywhere—at several locations in stations; on the sidewalks in front of tabacco shops and drug stores; in the lobbies or entranceways of office buildings, in coffee shops and numerous other places. They come in two sizes: "short" and "tall."

Some of the "tall" phones have a gold-colored band around them. These are for inter-city as well as local calls. They also accept only ¥10 coins—up to a maximum of six coins or ¥60.

Local calls on the red public telephones are limited to 3 minutes. When 2 minutes are up, a buzzer sounds. When 3 minutes are up, the connection is automatically broken. If you have not finished your conversation, you have to re-dial.

The rate for inter-city phone calls is determined by the distance between the two points. For example, it costs ¥10 to call Yokohama for a 50-second period. If you are calling Osaka, however, you get only 5 seconds for ¥10. To prevent the connection from being broken when you are making an inter-city call, you continue to drop ¥10 coins into the slot—while you are talking and before each time increment is up—to the maximum of six.

Reason for the restricted time limit on public phones is to prevent them from being tied up for long periods.

Some Useful Phone Numbers
Long Distance (Domestic): 100
Long Distance (Overseas): 109 in Tokyo
   Outside of Tokyo: 03-211-5511
Police: 110
Fire & Other Emergencies: 119

Plugging In

If you are traveling with, or buy, electrical appliances and accessories, keep in mind that 100 volts is standard throughout Japan, but the cycles differ in north and south. In the Tokyo area, the voltage is 50 cycles; in the Kyoto-Osaka district it is 60 cycles. Appliances set for 60 cycles are sluggish in the Tokyo area.

Beware of Stiff Shirts

Japanese drycleaners and laundries, particularly those affiliated with hotels, provide excellent and rapid service. Shirts are automatically starched unless you clearly specify otherwise.

Your Passport & Alien Registration Booklet

Japanese law states that visitors (as well as foreign residents) should carry their passports at all times—for quick, positive identification in case of an emergency. The law also requires that anyone, traveler as well as resident, who stays in Japan more than 60 days must obtain a special identification passbook called *Gaikokujin Toroku Shomeisho* (Alien Registration Booklet) from the ward office (or town or city office) of the area in which the person resides—or in the case of a tourist, where he is staying temporarily or is using as a mailing address.

Since the usual tourist visa for American citizens is good for only 60 days, this requirement applies only to travelers who extend their visas beyond the initial 60-day limit.

To extend your visa (for legitimate travel purposes), it is necessary to submit an application to the proper Immigration office 10 days before your original visa expires. In Tokyo this office is the *Tokyo Nyukoku Kanri Jimusho*, and it is located at 3-20, 1-chome Konan, Minato-ku. Tel. 471-5111. The office is almost always crowded, with lines in front of each window. Best idea is to send a messenger to the office in advance to obtain the application forms and instructions, and fill them out before you go there.

To obtain the Alien Registration Booklet, you need three photographs, passport size or a little smaller. The ID booklet is issued free, and usually takes only 15 to 20 minutes to obtain. If you plan to stay in Japan over 60 days, ask your hotel clerk, landlord, etc., for the location of the appropriate ward office.

Sizes, Weights & Distances in Japan

Japanese apparel sizes are based on the metric scale, in which 1-inch = 2.54 centimeters, and 1-centimeter = 0.39 inches. Women who wear a size 8 shoe in English need a size 26 in Japanese. For men, a shirt with a 15-inch neck becomes a size 38 in Japanese. A Japanese girl whose figure messures 76-50-81 in the metric system is a modest 30-20-32 in inches.

Weights in Japan are measured in grams. One pound = 0.4436 kilograms, and 1-kilogram = 2.2 pounds. Therefore, a 180-pound man weighs a little more than 81 kilograms.

Distances in Japan are measured in kilometers. One kilometer=0.62 miles; one mile= 1.60 kilometers. It is 318 miles or 514 kilometers from Tokyo to Kyoto.

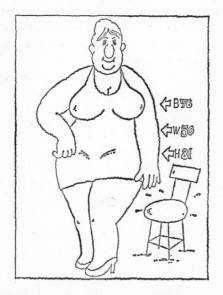

Credit Cards

Credit cards are widely used in Japan. The most popular of the American cards are Diner's Club, which is abbreviated as DC; and American Express, or AE. Bank Americard and Master Charge are also common.

Golden Week

Anyone in Japan or planning on being there during the first week of May should keep in mind that three national holidays occur during this period, with the result that public transportation systems and hotel-inn accommodations are exceptionally crowded with people taking advantage of the "Golden Week."

These holidays include the Emperor's Birthday on April 29, Constitution Day on May 3 and Children's Day on May 5. Not only do many people take extra days off during this period, business in general also slows down.

Any hotel or travel arrangements covering Golden Week should be made well in advance.

When Accosted By a Student. . . .

Most Japanese students study English, and many often have an overwhelming desire to try their English on Westerners. As a result, it is symptomatic for them to strike up conversations with visitors at street intersections, in shops, on trains, or wherever the opportunity presents itself.

Such students are especially apt to approach Western visitors who look lost or in need of some other kind of help. They therefore often give as much or more than they get.

In fact, it is commonplace for students to go considerably out of their way to help travelers, often aiding them with their shopping or guiding them to their destination—just for the opportunity to practice their English.

Many travelers approached in this manner have later reported the experience as one of the most pleasant they had in Japan.

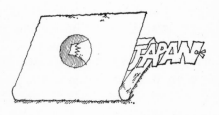

If You Get Sick

If you should suddenly become ill while you are in Japan, you can get excellent medical care. If you are at your hotel, simply call the front desk and ask the clerk to contact a doctor. All hotels have lists of available doctors.

If ambulance service and hospital arrangements are necessary, your hotel will also take care of these matters for you. If you are only a short distance away from your hotel and fall ill, return to the hotel if you can. If you cannot, ask someone to call the hotel for you and request whatever service you need.

If you are traveling with a group, your tour guide will see that you get immediate medical attention. If you are traveling without a guide, any policeman, shopkeeper, or anyone else for that matter, will help you.

If no one around you speaks English, just say the following: *Byoki desu. Oisha-san yonde kudasai* (Bee-yoe-key dess. Oh-ee-shah-sann yone-day coo-dah-sigh)—which means: "I'm sick, please call a doctor."

As for patent medicines, drug stores are more common in Japan than in the United States. They carry all the usual drugs and medicines as well as many antibiotics that can be obtained only with prescriptions in the United States.

In major Japanese cities there are usually one or more "American-style" pharmacies that carry drugs imported from the United States and other countries. The best-known of these in Tokyo is the *American Pharmacy*, in the northeast corner

of the Hibiya Park Building, two blocks north of
the Imperial Hotel. Telephone: 271-4034/5.

More on Money

Remember that once you are outside your
home country (or just your home city) personal
checks generally cannot be cashed without clear-
ance from your bank by letter or cable, and you
pay the charges.

It is best to have the bulk of your funds in
travelers' checks, keeping in mind that TC's in
smaller demoninations are often more appropriate for shopping.

Also keep in mind that not all shops, restaurants or inns (or lesser hotels in the prefec-
tures) accept travelers checks, and that cash
payment may be necessary. If you should find
yourself in this situation, you can cash your TC's
at the nearest Japanese bank.

PART II

GETTING THE MOST OUT OF YOUR YEN

How the Japanese Do It

For years a popular but frustrating pastime among foreign residents in Japan, particularly in Tokyo, has been trying to figure out how the Japanese can afford ("Especially on their *low* income!") to pay the "high" prices charged by well-patronized hotels, restaurants, shops, department stores, cabarets and other recreational facilities that abound in the major cities.

The answer to this apparent mystery is several-fold. The real income of workers in Japan, more often than not, is grossly underestimated, even by local residents, because only the so-called "base wages" are considered. In addition to their base pay, Japanese employees receive two substantial bonuses a year, several cash allowances, and various benefits in kind which, when added up, come close to doubling their income.

Besides this, income in Japan has been rising at a rate of 10 to 18 percent a year since the late 1950s. Prices have also gone up, of course, but at less than half this rate. The problem many foreign residents (and visitors as well) have in accepting prices in Japan today results from their not being able to fully rationalize and accept these changes. Their thinking tends to be fixed somewhere in the 1950s and early 60s, when most had a very significant financial advantage over the Japanese.

Another key factor in the ability of the Japanese to indulge in so much conspicuous consumption is that most of them spend considerably less of their income for housing and transportation than Americans do, for example. While Americans average spending about 20 to 25 percent of their total income on housing and another 10 to 15 percent on transportation, the typical Japanese spends about half as much on these two items.

Furthermore, and again particularly in Tokyo where prices are highest, a hefty percentage of Japan's "big spenders" is made up of the several hundred thousand families and individuals who are at the top of the country's economic ladder, and who constitute a large, affluent consuming market comparable to similarly elite groups in New York, London and Paris.

Then there are those fabulous expense account budgets most Japanese companies provide their executives, from section manager on up. Because of the deep-seated importance of entertainment in Japan's business world and relatively liberal tax write-off advantages, these expense account budgets amount to anywhere from a few hundred dollars to several thousand dollars a month per executive.

It is this large group, entertaining associates and clients, that fills Japan's thousands of plush bars and hostess cabarets each night, and with which the average foreign businessman or visitor should not try to compete.

Most Japanese, however—and by "most" I mean somewhere in the neighborhood of 75 percent—do *not* patronize conspicuously expensive places. They, like their counterparts in the U.S. and other highly affluent countries, must still economize. They too avoid the ritziest restaurants, the plushest and most expensive night clubs, the prestige department stores, the exclusive country-club jet-set style of life.

For the average foreign tourist or businessman visiting Japan today—as well as anyone else interested in exercising some restraint on their expenses—that is exactly what I recommend: that they take advantage of the accommodations, dining, shopping, entertainment and travel facilities patronized by ordinary middle-class and upper middle-class Japanese, at approximately the same middle and upper-middle class prices they would expect to pay for the same quality and service in the U.S., England or France.

There are, however, some differences between foreign visitors economizing in Japan, and avoiding rich-man prices in their own home country or more familiar travel areas. It is often difficult, and sometimes impossible, for the uninitiated visitor in Japan to determine in advance which restaurant, shop or club is going to be expensive, moderately priced or inexpensive. Both experience and familiar guidelines are missing.

My primary purpose here is to provide some of the more obvious of these missing guidelines, along with suggesting a number of options open to visitors who are willing to try something new.

Accommodations at Lower Prices

Again using New York, London and Paris as examples, the average visitor to these cities does not demand or expect to be put up in the plushest, most expensive hotel available. But that is precisely what happens to most travelers visiting Japan. They either request reservations at such places as Tokyo's famous Imperial Hotel, the Okura or the Tokyo Hilton, or their travel agent books them there automatically.

There are several other hotels in Tokyo substantially less expensive than the above three that are still first-class (deluxe in fact), where the variety and quality of the services compare with the best hotels in the U.S. and Europe.

For that matter, by international standards among highly advanced nations, hotel and inn accommodations in Japan are not priced out of line. Rooms at such super-deluxe hotels as the Imperial and Okura—even with the dollar substantially devalued—still begin at about $20 for singles and $30 for doubles.

Room charges at leading hotels in Osaka, Kyoto, Kobe and other important business and travel centers around the country are 10 to 25 percent lower than Tokyo rates. There are also many hotels in Tokyo as well as in other cities in Japan that are below the deluxe level but still first-class in every sense of the word. Then there are choices among second and third-class hotels that are more economical still—and usually just as clean and comfortable. Finally, there are the non-luxurious *ryokan* (Japanese inns), youth hostels, "People's Lodges," and National Vacation Villages.

The best thing for the traveler—tourist or businessman—planning a trip to Japan and interested in economizing on accommodations is to write, call or visit the nearest office of the *Japan National Tourist Organization* (JNTO), and ask for one or all of the following booklets (which the organization publishes and distributes free): *Japan Hotel Guide, Japan Ryokan Guide* and *Youth Hostels in Japan*.

The hotel guide gives specific prices and other information on over 250 hotels in the country, along with which of them offer off-season discounts. The ryokan guide lists 1,972 of the approximately 75,000 inns in the country—covering only those that are members of the *Japan Ryokan Association*, and are governed by strict rules regarding facilities and sanitary conditions.

Ryokan rates in popular resorts and major cities run from about ¥4,000 to ¥12,000 or more, depending on their quality, reputation and location. These rates usually include two meals (breakfast and supper), and are sometimes the same for one or two persons. Since the discount for ryokan accommodations without meals is generally only 15 percent, it is better to take the with-meals plan.

The youth hostel booklet lists 585 hostels scattered all over the country, and includes details on who is eligible to use them and the procedure for making reservations. Most of the hostels are new, well-constructed, and located in particularly scenic areas. A bed, two meals and use of the facilities runs about ¥1,000 a day.

More information about hosteling in Japan is available from: Japan Youth Hostels, Inc., Hoken Kaikan, 2, 1-chome, Sadohara-cho, Ichigaya, Shinjuku-ku, Tokyo, Japan. Tel. 269-5831.

In addition to these publications, available from JNTO offices around the world, the same organization's *Tourist Information Center* in Tokyo (Kotani Bldg., 1-chome, Yurakucho, Chiyoda-ku) also has available specially prepared supplementary sheets (mimeographed) listing "Reasonably Priced" hotels and inns in Tokyo and Kyoto.

The current listing covers 22 hotels, several lodges, centers, and houses in Tokyo; and 8 inns in Kyoto, plus one private home that takes in guests inn-style. Rates at these establishments range from 20 to 50 percent below those of regular hotels and inns.

Among the reasonably priced accommodations in Tokyo covered in the supplementary listings are the Shiba Park Hotel, San Bancho Hotel, Hotel Kokusai Kanko, Ginza Dai Ichi Hotel, Gajoen Kanko Hotel, Toshi Center, Hotel Tokyu Kanko, Hill Top Hotel, Nagara Inn, Shinriki Inn, and the Shinjuku Business Hotel.

Japan also boasts some 300 *Kokumin Shukusha*, or "People's Lodges," mostly situated in beautiful national parks, that are available to foreign visitors as well as Japanese. The large, barrack-like traveler accommodations, with bunk-style bedrooms, have two nightly rate structures, depending on the type of building. Rates for ferro-concrete buildings are slightly higher than those for buildings made of wood. Both are under $10 a night and include two meals.

Reservations at the Kokumin Shukusha can be made through offices of the Japan Travel Bureau, the travel sections of prefectural governments and city offices.

Another possibility for economical accommodations in Japan are the *Kokumin Kyuka Mura*, or National Vacation Villages. These villages, in national and quasi-national parks, are open to all, and include lodges, ski lifts, playgrounds, boating and camping sites, etc.

Reservations at National Vacation Villages can also be made through Japan Travel Bureau offices, or directly through the Tokyo Service Center of the National Vacation Village Corporation, c/o the Tokyo Kotsu Kaikan, 2-13 Yurakucho, Chiyoda-ku, Tokyo. Overnight rates, including two meals, are 20 to 40 percent less than typical hotel rates.

Those interested in additional information on the above facilities, or the publications named, are invited to contact the *Japan National Tourist Organization* main office or any of its overseas branches.

JNTO's head office is at 2-13 Yurakucho, Chiyoda-ku, Tokyo. The organization maintains 16 offices abroad, including six in the United States, at: 45 Rockefeller Plaza, New York, N.Y. 10020; 333 N. Michigan Ave., Chicago, Illinois, 60601; 1420 Commerce St., Dallas, Texas 75201; 1737 Post St., San Francisco, California 94115; 727 West 7th St., Los

Angeles, Calif., 90017; and 109 Kaiulani Ave., Honolulu, Hawaii 96815.

JNTO offices in other countries include: **Canada**—165 University Ave., Toronto 1, Ontario; **England**—167 Regent St., London W.1.; **Australia**—115 Pitt St., Sydney, N.S.W. 200; **Hong Kong**—Peter Building, 58 Queen's Rd.; and **Thailand**—56 Suriwong Rd., Bangkok.

Also: **France**—8 Rue de Richelieu, Paris; **Switzerland**—Rue de Berne 13, Geneve; **Germany**—Biebergasse 6-10, Frankfurt a/M; **Mexico** —Reforma 122, 5th piso, B-2, Mexico 6, D.F.; and **Brazil**—Ave. Paulista 1009, Ci-2003, Sao Paulo.

For those who like camping, the Seibu Railway Company operates lodges and tent-sites in some 15 of the mountainous areas of Okumusashi and Chichibu, northwest of Tokyo. Other Seibu camping sites include Lake Miyazawa, Shomaru Pass, Nakatsu Valley and Hino Valley.

The railway line's Nishi Chichibu Kesekien campgrounds on the Akahira River in Saitama Prefecture is open throughout the year, and offers bungalows for groups of three, four and six persons at low rates. Tents are also available.

For other information and reservations, call Seibu's tourism center at (03) 983-2155.

Japanese inns and hotels are legally permitted to charge a cancellation fee of up to 100 percent of the room cost if you make reservations and do not use them or cancel well in advance. If you make reservations and then cancel them five minutes later, there may be a charge of 10 to 20 percent of the total cost of the room.

If a travel agent makes reservations for you, the agency is held responsible for paying any cancellation fees. It is obviously best not to make reservations until your travel plans are definite, and to cancel as early as possible if for any reason the trip is called off.

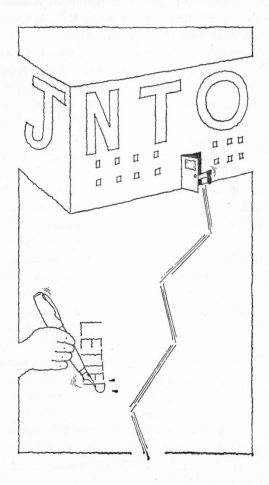

Eating Well on a Budget

Japan has more restaurants than any other country in the world (over 430,000), and richly deserves its well-established reputation as a gourmet's Shangri-La. What Japan does not deserve are the recent inferences that *all* eating out in Tokyo, Kyoto and other ranking Japanese cities is like buying into a gold mine.

There are expensive restaurants in Japan, particularly in Tokyo. But these extravagantly priced places are the exception, and again, have their counterparts in Paris and other cosmopolitan world cities (where people do not gasp in disbelief when they hear that dinner with drinks in an exclusive, posh eatery can run as high as $50 or more a head).

Most of the would-you-believe-it stories now circulating about the expense of eating out in Japan concern steak and other beef dishes in specialty restaurants and deluxe hotel dining rooms. A combination of increasing demand and decreasing supply has driven the cost of beef sky-high, and these prices are naturally reflected on the menus of restaurants that serve beef.

There has also been a steady annual rise in prices across the board for all commodities and services in Japan, with the result that Japan is not now, and has not been for many years, a "cheap" country. With this out of the way, let's take a look at how and where one can dine out in Japan today without having to hock the family jewels.

The first two things to keep in mind if you want

to eat at a reasonable cost in Japan is, of course, to avoid big steak/roast beef dinners altogether, especially in the specialty restaurants and deluxe hotel dining rooms already mentioned. For that matter, the economy-minded visitor or resident will avoid all hotel dining except for their coffee shops. These often have good breakfast and lunch choices at quite reasonable prices (except for coffee!).

The third rule in economic dining in Japan today is to avoid most of the other specialty shops that cater to well-to-do residents, tourists and the expense-account market. Prices in these places have always been premium; yen now costs dollar-spenders a great deal more than it used to, and such restaurants add a luxury tax of 10 to 15 percent to their bills—not to mention the "service charge" of another 10 to 15 percent tacked on in lieu of a tip.

So where does this leave the hungry traveler? With plenty of good food to eat at prices that are not outrageous, I assure you. For many visitors, however, taking advantage of lower priced restaurants in Japan is not that easy. It often requires a fairly substantial psychological shift. The visitor must accept the idea that he or she cannot eat economically in Japan while patronizing the most expensive restaurants in the country.

The economy-minded traveler must be willing to step off the gold-lined *Tourist Trail* and eat in the restaurants that most Japanese patronize—the traditional and popular *Osoba-ya*, *tempura-ya*, *tonkatsu-ya*, *kamameshi-ya*, *shokudo*, *chuka ryori-ya*, and so on. Before the traveler gnashes a gum, let me do a little explaining and translating.

There are three primary categories of food in Japan: Japanese, Western type, and Chinese. Within the Japanese category there are some 40 popular noodle dishes (*Osoba* and *udon*); over 25 equally popular rice dishes; and well over 100 specialty dishes made up of seafoods, vegetables, chicken, meat, roots, plants and combinations thereof.

There are three types of restaurants that serves these Japanese dishes: the *Osoba-ya* ("ya" means "shop" or "place") which sells noodle dishes; the *koryori-ya*, which offers an amazing variety of seafood, vegetable and part-meat dishes; and the famous *Osushi-ya*, which specialize in slices of raw fish and other fresh seafoods served on buns of seasoned rice.

A fourth type of restaurant, usually thought of as Japanese, is the ubiquitous *shokudo* (something like an American cafeteria or short-order restaurant) which serves a choice of the most popular Japanese, Western type and Chinese dishes.

Japan has two types of Chinese restaurants—the very common neighborhood family-type known as *chuka ryori-ya* (Chinese food place), which serves inexpensive "Japanese versions" of well-known Chinese dishes; and the relatively exclusive and more expensive Chinese-operated Chinese restaurants that cater to foreign residents, visitors, cosmopolitan Japanese *and* Chinese.

Then there are numerous non-exclusive spe-

cialty houses, usually small and often very pic-
turesque, mainly serving one particular kind of
food at prices that go from inexpensive and
moderate to expensive.

The less expensive of these specialty shops,
which means those that cater to ordinary Japanese, include *yakitori-ya* (specialists in chunks of
chicken charcoal broiled on skewers and dipped
in sauce); *tempura-ya* (seafood and vegetables
dipped in a special batter and deep-fried; *tonkatsu-ya* (pork tenderloin cutlets breaded and
deep-fried); and *kamameshi-ya* (rice steamed in
fish bouillon seasoned with soy sauce and laced
with small bits of chicken, pork, or mushrooms,
plus bamboo shoots, peas, etc.)

Noodles, one of the most popular snack and
lunch choices in Japan, are either Japanese style
—with the two most popular being *soba* (long,
brownish-grey and made of buckwheat flour) and
udon (long, white and made of wheat flour)—or
Chinese (long and yellowish).

Japanese-style noodles are usually served in
soup stock and garnished with slivers of meat,
seafood and/or vegetables. They are a specialty
of the *Osoba-ya*, the *udon-ya* and the *shokudo*.
Chinese noodles, eaten boiled or fried and usually
with a vegetable/meat mixture (like chow mein),
are found in *chuka ryori-ya* and *shokudo*.

The next big category of food is the many
rice dishes, served mostly in *shokudo* and *chuka
ryori-ya*, consisting of plates or bowls of rice
topped with such things as pork, shrimp, crab,
beef stew, curry-flavored stew, etc.

How do visitors find these restaurants? They

are almost everywhere! Invariably there are anywhere from one or two to a dozen or more of
each category clustered around train stations (of
which there are over 75 in Tokyo). Entertainment
and shopping districts also have their own collec-
tion of restaurants. All department stores and
many office buildings have one to half a dozen
general and specialty restaurants on their pre-
mises.

"Local" restaurants are usually easy to recognize because most of them have authentic-
looking wax models of their dishes in glassed-in
display windows or cases; outside or just inside
their entrances. Prices are displayed with these
replicas so the diner can decide on what he wants
and know how much it is going to cost before
sitting down. Many other non-exclusive restaurants have their menus and prices prominent-
ly displayed outside for the convenience of
patrons.

Besides the thousands of individual restaurants
in Japan, there are also a number of chain restaurants that serve good Western-type food at
moderate prices—and seldom become known to
the typical tourist or visiting businessman. These
include the Fujiya chain, the Morinaga, Meiji
and the Benihana chains; also the Aka Hyotan
Salad Shops, the Acacia Salad Shops, the Coqd'or
restaurant chain, and the Tivoli (Italian) food
shops.

Coffee shops and snack restaurants also
abound in Japan, and do a thriving business during breakfast, lunch and after hours. They mainly
serve toast, eggs, coffee, sandwiches, soft drinks,

pastries and a few short-orders a'la the *shokudo*. Coffee, tea and soft drinks are the most expensive items (for what you get) on coffee shop-and-snack restaurant menus.

And, of course, there are the growing-in-popularity convenience restaurants — MacDonald's, Kentucky Fried Chicken, Dunkin Donuts, the Pioneer Take Out Sandwich Shops, and others in the same category. Many shokudo-type restaurants in or adjoining commutor train stations feature what is called "Morning Service," which consists of a breakfast of eggs and/or toast and coffee at low prices.

Finally, the visitor who fails to buy and try Japan's delicious breads and pastries is missing a rare treat. Bakeries, some of them also national chains, can be found in most shopping centers, entertainment and restaurant districts, as well as in department stores. Bread varieties include French, Russian and German, and the choice of pastries seems endless. Bakery chain names to keep in mind: Fujiya, Kimura-ya, German Bakery, Yamazaki-ya and Coqd'or Vienna Bread.

Many hotel rooms in Japan come equipped with refrigerators. Experienced travelers, myself included, make a practice of stocking them with such items as milk, fruit, luncheon meats, rolls, honey *and* peanut butter—all obtained at nearby supermarkets.

Seeing the "Real" Japan for Less

Visitors to Japan are often trapped on a tourist treadmill that locks them in on the same premium-priced hotels, shops, restaurants, events and scenes; with few options for experiencing traditional Japan or for keeping their expenses below astronomical figures.

As it happens, the Japan that most visitors really want to see and experience can only be glimpsed in Tokyo, Osaka and other major business centers—where prices are naturally the highest. Thus the traveler wanting to stretch his yen in Japan can combine economizing with getting off the *Tourist Trail* and enjoying close, personal contact with "un-Westernized" Japanese and their culture.

How can this be done? By putting up in smaller, neighborhood hotels, inns and other kinds of lodging; by eating in restaurants patronized by ordinary local residents; by utilizing local commutor transportation systems, and by spending less time in the large, Westernized cities.

We have already discussed moderately priced lodgings and dining in detail, so let's look at the next two areas of concern: transportation, and where to spend your time in Japan to get the most out of your trip for the least money.

Most of Japan's larger cities have several types of transportation: private hire limousines, taxis, subways, city trains, buses and interurban trains. Private limousines are out for the budget-minded traveler. Taxis are not particularly expensive by international standards—averaging about 75 cents a mile—and they are especially practical most of the time.

Major hotels, train stations, and some department stores and office buildings have taxi stands adjoining their front entrances. Cruising cabs are plentiful, except when it rains and demand for them doubles or triples. They will stop almost anywhere for a fare—except when the hundreds of bars and clubs close between 11 and 11:30 p.m. and their thousands of patrons stream out looking for taxis to take them home. At this time, taxi drivers in or near the entertainment areas will often refuse to pick passengers up unless they agree in advance to pay more than the meter shows.

In addition to this, taxi fares officially go up 20 percent after 11 p.m. Late at night, then, especially in or near entertainment districts, taxis can be quite expensive.

For the budget-watcher, however, Japan's subways, buses and trains are real yen stretchers. Stations and stops are numerous and conveniently located near, under, on or in hotels, shopping centers, entertainment districts, department stores, parks, recreational facilities and important government and private buildings.

In Tokyo, for example, there are seven subway lines which criss-cross the city in an irregular spoke fashion, and come together, or within a few hundred feet of each other (with connecting underground passageways), in the central portion of the downtown area.

The subway stations are clean and well-illuminated. Most have their signs in both Japanese and English. The trains run every 2 to 5 minutes from early morning until just after midnight. Tickets are sold through automatic vending machines, and large posted graphs in each station show all the different routes, stations and fares to specific destinations.

Besides Tokyo, Osaka, Nagoya and Sapporo have subway lines. Sapporo, in fact, boasts a subway that runs on rubber wheels, greatly reducing the noise factor.

Local commutor trains, particularly in the Tokyo and Osaka areas, compete with the subways in convenience, efficiency and economy. Tokyo has one great Loop Line (*Yamanote-sen*) that circles the city's heart. The city is also disected from east to west by the *Chuo-sen* (Central Line) and from north to south by the *Keihin Line*—all of which have several interconnecting stations.

In addition to these public inner-city train lines, there are also several privately operated inter-urban lines that originate at various public-line terminals in Tokyo and go to outlying wards of the sprawling capital—as well as to neighboring towns, cities and nearby resorts like Hakone, Nikko and Kamakura. All of these lines provide rapid, efficient and inexpensive service; with trains coming into and leaving stations like clockwork, at intervals of 2 to 5 minutes, depending on the time of day.

Trains on all of the lines are very crowded from about 7:30 to 9:30 a.m. and again from 5 to 7 p.m. But during the remaining hours, they take both the pain and expense out of traveling about in one of the world's most densely populated and complicated urban areas.

Tokyo and other Japanese cities also have extensive local bus networks. They too are inexpensive, dependable and convenient, especially for reaching destinations between subway and train stations—although they are not as fast as other methods of transportation. But the traveler must have some language ability, above average courage and a special knack for navigating through the city labyrinths to take advantage of Japan's buses, because all of the bus-stop signs and destination signs on the buses are in Japanese only, and drivers cannot be expected to speak English.

Of course, Japan's long-distance trains, especially the "Bullet" expresses that run between Tokyo, Nagoya, Kyoto, Osaka and Okayama, are internationally famous. Not only are they fast (average speed is 120 mph) and convenient (departures and arrivals every 15 minutes), they are also inexpensive. The fare between Tokyo and Osaka (556.4 kilometers) is under $20 on the *Hikari* trains, which stop only at Nagoya and Kyoto; and less on the *Kodama* trains, which make 12 stops on the way to Osaka.

The extra charge for a reserved seat on either of the two Bullet Expresses is under 50 cents. The first of the super express trains leaves Tokyo at 6 a.m. every morning, and the last train leaves Osaka for Tokyo at 8:30 p.m. every evening.

In addition to the Hikari and Kodama super express trains, there are numerous other, slower, limited express trains leaving various terminals in Tokyo at short intervals for other parts of the islands; along with branch lines radiating out from other major cities into the countryside.

Route maps, time-tables, prices and other information on Japan's transportation systems are available from Japan Travel Bureau Offices, from the *Tourist Information Center* (TIC) in Tokyo (1-chome, Yurakucho), in TIC branch centers at Tokyo International Airport (also called *Haneda*) and the Kyoto Tower Building in Kyoto, and from *Japan National Tourist Organization* offices around the world (listed earlier).

Train reservations should be made at least three weeks in advance for travel to summer resorts during the summer and to winter resorts during the winter. It is also important to make reservations well in advance if you want to travel over three-day weekends or holiday periods, such as *Golden Week* in May when there are three national holidays in one week, *Obon* in July, and the last several days preceding New Years.

Reserved train tickets may be cancelled up to two days before travel time with only a small service charge. Anyone who cancels later than this but before train time is usually charged 30 percent of the fare. Anyone who fails to cancel may be charged the full fare.

"Non-tourist" touring is old hat in Europe. Initially started by young people who couldn't afford to pay going rates at leading tourist facilities, the concept was later adopted by older, Establishment-types who finally realized that getting away from the big cities and into the countryside was where it was at.

This type of touring in Japan is popular among the Japanese but is still to come into its own where foreign travelers are concerned. It is, however, what I suggest for those who are sincerely interested in getting the most out of their Japan experience at a reasonable cost.

Besides lodging facilities and restaurant prices being cheaper in Japan's smaller cities—particularly those not professionally developed as tourist attractions—it is in the outlying towns and villages of Japan that one finds the unspoiled, stunning natural beauty, the exotic costumes and traditional everyday life-styles which have given Japan such a fascinating image in the first place.

But to break away from the crowd this way requires, again, something special. There is a strong tendency for the travel industry to keep the visitor on the familiar, "safe" *Tourist Track* ("for their own good," of course)—and the industry has an important point.

Just the language problem alone could defeat most visitors trying to take care of themselves in an isolated non-tourist setting. The sensible thing is not to go too far; to forego the gold-plated amenities of the big tourist-oriented cities for others that are substantially less expensive, and yet are often more attractive and rewarding.

A week spent on the northern island of Hokkaido, for example, is a treat so unusual for Tokyo residents today that those who manage to go there on vacation or business trips are invariably enraptured by the experience. Prices there range from 20 to 50 percent below those in Tokyo.

A visit to the other end of Japan, to Kagoshima on the southern tip of Kyushu, is like taking a huge step back into time, not only in the quality and style of life, but also in prices.

In between these two geographic extremes are numerous other cities of extraordinary historical interest—most with nearby scenic wonders that have been nationally famous for centuries; noted hotspring resorts, inns and hotels so far patronized mostly by Japanese; all bustling with their own shopping and entertainment districts, and all conveniently accessible by air and train from Japan's major ports of entry.

These cities include Sapporo and Chitose in Hokkaido; Aomori, Morioka, Akita, Sendai and Niigata in the northern part of the main island of Honshu; Yokohama, Kanazawa, Toyama, Gifu, Nagoya and Shizuoka in central Honshu; Okayama, Matsue and Hiroshima on sourthern Honshu; any of the larger towns on the little island of Shikoku; and, Nagasaki, Kumamoto, Oita and Fukuoka on the southern island of Kyushu—to name just a few of the dozens.

Tokyo's Monorail

Tokyo's well-known monorail runs from Hamamatsucho in central Tokyo to a below-ground terminal in the Departure Building at Tokyo International Airport. Trains depart every 10 minutes; the trip—part of it over Tokyo Bay—takes 15 minutes. One-way fare is ¥190.

Hamamatsucho, where the monorail begins and ends, is the third station south of Tokyo Central Station—about 6 or 8 minutes—on either the Yamanote Loop Line or the Keihin Line, which parallel each other at this point.

Biggest disadvantage of the monorail for departing and arriving air passengers is the necessity for lugging one's baggage around. There is no space provided on the trains for baggage (the seats are small), and no porter service at either end of the line. Departing passengers who do take the monorail have to carry their luggage several hundred feet from where they disembark to the airline check-in counters.

Bargain Buying in Japan

Despite past monetary fluctuations and rising prices in general, Japan still offers many shopping bargains—in cameras, camera equipment, hi-fi sets, miniature TV sets, radios, and so on. Then of course there are the numerous non-competitive traditionally style items made in Japan: lacquerware, ceramics, earthenware, ivory carvings, silks, woodblock prints, brocades, pearls, etc.

At the same time, there are a number of ways for visitor-shoppers to make sure they are getting every possible price advantage. Probably the most important of these is to make your purchases, whenever possible, in so-called "Tax-Free" shops. These are shops designated by the National Tax Office to sell certain items tax-free to visitors who are in the country on tourist visas.

Only certain categories of merchandise are eligible for tax-exempt sales. These include articles made of or decorated with precious stones or semiprecious stones; pearls and articles made of or decorated with pearls; articles made of precious metals, decorated with gold or platinum and plated or covered with precious metals; articles made of tortoise shell, coral, amber and ivory; cloisonne ware; furs; household implements made of fiber; portable TV sets; record players and stereo equipment.

Also, radios; magnetic tape recorders; cameras, movie cameras and projectors, including parts and accessories; slide projectors; and watches and clocks when the cases are decorated with precious stones or semi-precious stones.

The savings at tax-free shops amounts to 10 percent on such popular items as radios and tape recorders, and 15 percent on cameras, record players, movie cameras and stereo equipment. On some items, the savings is 30 percent.

Tax-Free Shops are located in leading hotel arcades, and in the most popular shopping centers and districts. They have Tax-Free Shop signs conspicuously displayed at or near their entrances. Altogether, there are 1,315 of these shops in Japan—170 of them in Okinawa, and most of the remainder concentrated in Tokyo, Osaka and Kyoto.

To qualify for the tax exemption, visitors must have their passports on hand, and sign a "tax exempt certificate" which the shop provides and fills out at the time of purchase. The shopper gets a copy of the certificate to turn into Japanese Customs when leaving Japan.

Keep in mind that not all of the shops in hotel arcades are Tax-Free, and not all items in Tax-Free Shops come under the exemption. Also keep in mind that the base prices of items in shops located in deluxe hotels tend to be higher than in outside shops. But don't discount the possibility that the convenience of the hotel arcade shops may be worth more than the time and/or taxi fare it takes to go to an outside shop.

Most visitors, it seems, are inclined to do their shopping in Tokyo almost immediately after they arrive in Japan. Fairly substantial savings can be had by doing some of your shopping in lower priced areas, and by buying closer to the source. For example, Noritake china, produced in Nagoya, can be bought at the factory at big savings. Pearls are cheaper at the pearl farms in Toba than they are in Tokyo. Kyoto is a brocade producing center, so brocade prices are naturally cheaper there.

The *Japan National Tourist Organization*, mentioned earlier, publishes a shopping directory (*Souvenirs of Japan*), available free from its offices around the world, which lists recommended shops by category of merchandise throughout the country, and notes whether they are designated Tax-Free Shops. The booklet also lists the locally produced items that are the best buys in Tokyo, Yokohama, Nikko, Kyoto, Kobe, Osaka, Nagoya and Sapporo.

The *Japan Quality Store Association*, which has members in the popular travel cities, produces and distributes free (also through JNTO offices), a shopper's map showing the location of member-shops, with their addresses in both English and Japanese—the latter for taxi directions.

Finally, bargaining for discounts below the tax-free (or with-tax) price is no longer out of place in most tourist shops in Japan, particularly in those outside the hotel arcades. I also recently had the experience of a department store giving a discount without being asked for it, simply because of a rather large purchase.

Best idea if you are traveling with friends is to go to the same shop together and bargain for a group discount. Some good-humored enthusiasm in this direction will often go a long way.

The Traveler's Friend

The best source of both general and specific information on any aspect of accommodations and touring in Japan is the *Tourist Information Center* (TIC) in the Kotani Building at 1 Yuraku-cho, Chiyoda-ku, Tokyo.

Operated by the *Japan National Tourist Organization*, the TIC is staffed by English and French-speaking personnel, and acts as a free distribution point for English-language magazines, booklets, maps, pamphlets and brochures on a wide range of subjects of interest to visitors.

The TIC also maintains extensive files on tourism facilities, and undertakes to answer inquiries on-the-spot as well as by phone and mail—which means travelers planning on visiting Japan may write for information in advance.

Among other services provided by TIC are arranging for home-visits and licensed guides, and showing travel films. The center is open from 9 a.m. to 5 p.m. daily except Sundays and national holidays. The office closes from noon to 1 p.m. for lunch. Telephone numbers are: 503-2911 and 503-2926.

TIC branch centers are located in the Terminal Building at Tokyo International Airport (Haneda), Tel. 747-0261/2; and in the Kyoto Tower Building, Higashi Shiokoji-cho, Shimo-gyo-ku, Kyoto, tel. 371-0480.